THE ITTY BITTY GUIDE TO
business travel

THE ITTY BITTY GUIDE TO
business travel

BY STACIE KRAJCHIR
AND CARRIE ROSTEN

CHRONICLE BOOKS
SAN FRANCISCO

Text copyright © 2004 by Stacie Krajchir and Carrie Rosten. All rights reserved. No part of this book may be reproduced in any form without written permission from the publisher.

Library of Congress Cataloging-in-Publication Data available.

ISBN: 0-8118-4101-4

Manufactured in China

Designed by Ayako Akazawa

Distributed in Canada by Raincoast Books
9050 Shaughnessy Street
Vancouver, British Columbia V6P 6E5

10 9 8 7 6 5 4 3 2 1

Chronicle Books LLC
85 Second Street
San Francisco, California 94105
www.chroniclebooks.com

Dedication

To our families, for expanding our horizons and giving us the opportunity to travel.

Acknowledgments

To our editor at Chronicle Books, Mikyla Bruder, for her patience, guidance, and support in getting this book to where it needed to be and for co-piloting the Itty Bitty series. Grateful thanks to our legal leader and dear friend Nikki Harvat, for her continued support and guidance through each of our creative ventures. To Nicole Simons, who shared her incredible corporate travel insight and experience on so many levels, thank you. Grateful thanks to Shelby Meade, whose transcontinental travel-experience contributions and firsthand examples helped shape this book. To Sue and Richard, for providing us with enough international travel and "hotel life" advice to know exactly how to write so many parts of this book. Thanks to Leslie Davisson, part of Chronicle Books' behind-the-scenes A-team, who took on and walked us through so many itty bitty details, and helped get the book to the finish line. To our wonderful friends and families, who continuously support us. Thank you for being there for us and inspiring us always, especially Clarene, Alex, Sue, Nana, Papa, Richard, Carol, Nickie, Denny, Jackie, Pam, Andres, Maxwell, and Princess.

contents

Introduction 8

001 **Before You Book** 10
- UNDERSTAND YOUR TRIP 11
- KNOW YOUR COMPANY'S TRAVEL POLICIES 13
- MAP YOUR DESTINATION 20

002 **Booking Your Trip** 24
- USING A TRAVEL AGENT VERSUS SELF-BOOKING 25
- BOOKING YOUR FLIGHT 28
- BOOKING YOUR HOTEL 31
- GROUND TRANSPORTATION 36
- MAXIMIZING PERKS 38

003 Before You Go 42
- PREPARING YOUR OFFICE 43
- PREPARING YOUR HOME 54
- PREPARING YOUR MIND AND BODY 58

004 Packing Like a Pro 62
- PLAN BEFORE YOU PACK 63
- WHAT TO PACK 66
- HOW TO PACK LIKE YOU MEAN BUSINESS 71

005 Getting There 76
- TRANSPORTATION TO THE AIRPORT OR TRAIN STATION 77
- CHECKING IN FOR YOUR FLIGHT 82
- I'VE CHECKED IN . . . NOW WHAT? 86
- ON BOARD 90

006 You've Arrived 92
- TRANSPORTATION TO THE HOTEL 93
- CHECKING IN AT THE HOTEL 96
- HOME AWAY FROM HOME 101

007 Out and About 104
- GOING ABOUT YOUR BUSINESS 105
- TAKING TIME TO PLAY 108

008 Coming Home 112
- BEFORE YOU CHECK OUT 113
- CHECKING OUT OF THE HOTEL 117
- COMING HOME 121

Index 126

About the Authors 128

introduction

Whether you are heading out for a whirlwind week of research and networking, or zipping in and zipping out for a quick strategy meeting, the tips in *The Itty Bitty Guide to Business Travel* will help you make the most of your trip.

Find out how to plan a great business trip. You'll learn how to get a handle on your trip goals, prepare your colleagues for your absence, find the best travel deals and business hotels, pack like a pro, and make your hotel room a relaxing retreat. Lists of helpful questions will ensure that you're armed with the information you need, while handy checklists make it easy for you to get yourself and your belongings out the door on time.

Oh, that cramped airplane seat. That rich restaurant food. That uncomfortable hotel bed. If you think it's impossible to nap on the plane, eat properly while traveling, and sleep well in your hotel bed, think again. *The Itty Bitty Guide to Business Travel* offers some lifesaving tools and strategies for making your journey a truly healthy, restful, and productive one.

When the trip is over, the work has really just begun. Tips for organizing your thoughts, your notes, and your receipts will help you clear your mind before landing back on home turf. Advice for the return trip home will have you reentering your office with a clear mind and a rested body.

Get ready to become a savvy business traveler!

001

before you book

The seasoned business traveler knows that good planning paves the way to a more successful and less stressful business trip. By planning ahead and taking the time to really understand the reasons for the trip, you can accomplish the goals you set out to achieve in less time, spend less money, and maybe even earn a few perks and upgrades along the way. So before you even pick up the phone to book your next trip, spend some time getting a firm grasp on why you're going, where you're going, and what exactly you're expected to achieve.

The advice in this chapter covers those important details you need to consider before you book a flight or hotel. From understanding the purpose of your trip to learning your company's travel policies, here are the first steps to conducting effective and pleasurable business travel.

understand your trip

First things first: Understanding your goals is essential to a successful business trip. Goals can range widely, from finding a potential client to closing a protracted deal. To make sure you understand the objectives of your own trip, run down the following list of questions with your supervisor or colleagues. Take time to really understand the answers.

* **Why am I going on this trip and what am I expected to achieve?**

If you don't fully understand what is expected of you, it is likely that you won't achieve it. If the goal of your trip is to walk away with a deal, make sure you have a plan for making that deal happen.

* **With whom will I be meeting?**

Find out as much as you can about the people you're meeting with. Have these people met with anyone else from your company? If so, find out your colleagues' impressions of the persons involved. What will be expected of you? If you're going there to close a deal, are you meeting with the person who has the authority to sign on the dotted line?

* Where am I going?

The answer to this question is not just the address, city, and state, but also any inside information you can get. What's this place like? If you're going for just one meeting in one office, what's the office environment like? Casual? Formal? If you'll be attending many meetings all over town, what's the city like? Is public transportation easy to use, or will you be cabbing it everywhere? Do whatever research is necessary for you to really understand your destination.

* When do I need to be there?

Sure, it may seem obvious, but make sure you have your dates straight. Timing is crucial. If you're going for a conference, make sure you know the correct start and end times. If you'll be attending an important meeting, make certain that the people who need to be there are available when you are. Also, confirm that you and your supervisor are in agreement about how long you'll be away from the office.

know your company's travel policies

Talk to your human resources department or your supervisor about your company's official travel policies. It's extremely important that you know and understand the company guidelines before you book your trip. You'll save yourself time, and you'll save your company money. Following is a list of questions to review with your supervisor or human resources manager.

✱ What is the company per diem?

This daily allowance is meant to cover your necessary expenses, including food, lodging, transportation, and business-related entertainment. The per diem is not intended for personal use (a relaxing trip to the cinema with friends won't qualify), and it shouldn't be used for anything outside the realm of your business-related needs.

✻ Who is the company's preferred travel agent?

Many companies book all of their travel through a particular travel agency. Some companies even have a preferred airline or hotel chain. By using one such vendor they can often get a company-wide discount on air travel or hotel charges. Make sure you know your company's preferences before you book.

✻ If I book my own trip, what is my total trip budget?

It's good to know, before you start spending the company's money, how much they expect to pay for your trip. They should be able to give you an estimate for travel and hotel costs.

BE A CONSCIENTIOUS spender

Business travel is both a responsibility and a privilege. In sending you on this trip, your employer is entrusting you not only with the responsibility of achieving the goals of your trip but also with the care and keeping of the firm's money. You will be judged on how you handle this aspect of your job, so treat your employer's money with the same care as you treat your own.

TRAVELING with class

Let's face it, cramped quarters stink. If your company allows you to travel business class, consider yourself lucky. The extra amenities, work space, and legroom can make every difference in how you feel upon arrival, both mentally and physically.

However, the fact that your officemate flies business class doesn't mean your company will pay for you to fly business class, too. It is essential that you ask your supervisor what the company policy is before you book a business-class ticket. You certainly don't want to receive an unanticipated bill on your desk at a later date. Not only would this be a shock to your checkbook but it would also make you look unprofessional. If your company won't pick up the bill for a business-class ticket, you may be able to spend your own miles from your personal frequent-flier account to upgrade on a long cross-country or international flight. This personal expenditure will certainly pay for itself ten times over if it means you arrive well rested and relaxed.

✸ What expenses will I be reimbursed for?

In addition to the dollar limit on your per diem, your human resources manager can tell you exactly what kinds of expenses qualify for reimbursement. Make a photocopy of your company's travel policies and keep it with you.

✸ How do I get reimbursed?

Make sure you understand not only what expenses qualify for reimbursement but also the formal procedures for reimbursement. Most companies require receipts for everything over a certain dollar amount. Know that dollar amount, and plan to collect receipts accordingly. Plan to keep an expense log throughout your trip so you can keep track of every single expense, from the newspaper you buy at the airport to the catering bill for the power breakfast you host.

✸ Do I get reimbursed for tips?

Because tips don't always appear on receipts, ask about the policy for tip reimbursement.

Before you book your trip, consider whether you can stay for a few extra days or through the weekend, especially if your business will be concluded on a Thursday or Friday. Do you really have to report back at work right away or could you update your coworkers by e-mail instead? A lot of work can be done away from the office provided you have a laptop, Internet access, and a cell phone—and provided your absence isn't causing your coworkers to work late into the night covering your responsibilities. This may be the perfect opportunity to see a place you've always been curious about, meet up with old friends, or make new ones. Wouldn't it be so much nicer to write up that client's report while lounging on the beach than sitting in a stuffy cubicle? Go! You deserve an adventure.

EXTENDING YOUR TRIP for pleasure

✳ May I use vacation days to extend my trip?

Before you ask this question, find out whether you have vacation time coming to you. And be sensitive to the fact that your absence from the office may be a hardship on your colleagues. If you intend to extend your trip for vacation purposes, arrange for someone to cover your duties during your absence.

✳ May I use a company credit card?

Some companies prefer that employees use a company credit card for preapproved large expenses. Ask your supervisor or human resources department about the firm's credit card policy.

✳ Will I need to use my personal credit card?

If you are asked to use a personal credit card to pay for reimbursable expenses, confirm that your card's limit is high enough to cover all of your travel costs, including any unexpected expenses that may become necessary.

✹ Can I get a cash advance?

Some firms will give employees a cash advance so they don't have to go out-of-pocket for the expense of business travel. Business travel should not be a personal financial hardship. Talk to your supervisor or human resources department about alternatives.

Whether you're working for someone else or for yourself, use a separate credit card devoted only to business expenditures. Doing so makes tax-return preparation and accounting much easier.

SIMPLIFY YOUR spending

map your destination

Get the lay of the land before you book your travel. Knowing a little about your destination can help prevent some common business travel mishaps, such as flying into the wrong airport, booking a hotel that's hours away from your meeting place, or choosing an extremely expensive restaurant for a casual business lunch. Here are some suggestions for doing preliminary fact-finding about your destination.

GET A MAP

Whether downloaded from the Internet or purchased from a travel store, a good map is a crucial tool for the savvy business traveler. Use a colored pen to mark your map with your meeting places. Note the closest airports, preferred hotels, recommended restaurants, and any public transportation information.

ASK AROUND

It's likely that one of your colleagues has traveled to your destination and can provide you with the inside scoop on the best restaurants and bars and the ins and outs of public transportation.

GET ONLINE

Many chambers of commerce, local weekly papers, and city visitor's guides offer great online resources that can help you find out about everything from the weather to restaurant and hotel recommendations to current events.

> If you're nervous about making small talk, give yourself a crash course on local current affairs. Armed with a few good questions, you won't have to do all the talking. Research online, or clip newspaper or magazine articles to read on the plane. If the city you're visiting has a weekly or monthly publication, try to get hold of a recent copy.

MAKING SMALL talk

INTERNATIONAL travel

Traveling abroad requires extra care in planning ahead. It's especially important to research your destination. Before you book an international business trip, make sure you know the answers to the following questions:

Do I have a current passport?

If you need to renew your passport, you may be able to apply by mail. Check out http://travel.state.gov for more information on the process. If you need to obtain a new passport, you can download and complete the application before applying in person at your local passport agency. If you need a passport in a hurry (e.g., your boss has asked you to attend an international conference that starts in three weeks and your passport is expired), call your passport agency to make an appointment; show up with your tickets or airline-generated itinerary in hand, as well as any other required items. To receive a passport in about two weeks, you'll be required to pay an additional fee (as well as overnight-shipping charges).

Does my destination require a visa?
Call the local consulate of the country you'll need to travel to for details. The visa application process can take up to three months, so plan ahead. It is recommended that you apply for a visa in person at the consulate.

Do I need any vaccines to travel to my destination?
Again, contact the local consulate for the most current information on suggested or required vaccines. If you need any vaccines, see your doctor.

Has my government issued any travel warnings about my destination?
Before you book your travel arrangements, contact the U.S. Department of State (or visit http://travel.state.gov) and ask for the consular information sheet for the country you plan to visit.

booking your trip

002

Once you are confident that you understand your role and the purpose of your trip, it's time for you to book your travel and hotel. How well you care for the company's money may be interpreted as representing how much you care about your job, so it's important that you find a good deal. However, it's equally important that you travel in relative comfort. The more relaxed and comfortable you are, the more successful your trip will be. Covering flight, hotel, and ground transportation, as well as advice on using an agent and self-booking, this chapter will help you get what you want for less.

using a travel agent versus self-booking

There are definite advantages to booking a trip through an old-fashioned travel agent. An agent can help you secure a last-minute ticket and book your flight and hotel room all at once. He or she also has access to deals that simply aren't available to the general public. And, if you're using your company's preferred agent, not only will you benefit from the convenience of working with a tried-and-trusted party, but you also probably won't have to pay out-of-pocket for the ticket and hotel bill. Agents can be very helpful when your travel plans change unexpectedly. Instead of spending precious hours on the phone rebooking your flight and hotel, you can place just one call to your agent and allow him or her to take care of the details.

At the same time, some of the best hotel rates and flight fares can be found online. The Internet offers fast and direct access to links and sites that help you quickly compare prices for flights, hotels, and car rentals. Booking your own travel can mean a little more labor on your part. But if you're willing to put in that extra time, you're likely to find a pretty good deal. Be aware that travel Web sites sometimes feature deals that the hotel or airline reservation desk may not be privy to, and vice versa.

Even if your firm's travel agent is researching airfares and hotels for you, it's not a bad idea to do some online comparing. If you see a better rate than the one found by the travel agent, bring that information to the attention of your supervisor or human resources manager. There is a chance that they will still want you to book through the company agent,

> **WEATHER check**
>
> Before booking a flight find out the weather conditions at your destination and plan your route accordingly. For example, if you need to fly to New York and stormy weather is anticipated on Wednesday, consider flying in on Tuesday to beat the weather or delaying your trip until the storm has passed. Knowing weather conditions can also help you select a layover city—obviously, choose the layover city with the better weather.

since the group discount may constitute better savings in the long run, but you will have demonstrated that you care about the firm's best interests.

FINDING YOUR own agent

If your company does not use a travel agency, and you simply don't have the time to book your own travel, a good agent is not difficult to find. Ask friends and colleagues, particularly those who travel frequently, to recommend an agent who specializes in business travel. A good agent is a good listener. Easy to get hold of, she returns your calls quickly and is willing to get to know you and your travel needs. If you travel frequently, your agent should create and keep on file your travel profile, which includes your food, seating, lodging, and transportation preferences, as well as information about your company's travel policies and any pertinent restrictions. This customized profile allows the agent to try to book the seat you prefer, the hotel room you like, and the car you enjoy driving whenever you call for travel arrangements.

booking your flight

Whether you book through an agent or directly with an airline, it's helpful to jot down your preferences—direct flight, preferred airline, coach or business class, aisle or window seat, desired departure and arrival time, and price range—before you place the call. Once you have a ticket agent on the line, here are some of the questions you may need to ask.

- **Do you offer a corporate discount?**
- **Are alternative times or days cheaper?**
- **Would it be cheaper to fly into a different airport? Connect in an alternative city?**
- **What are the restrictions? When do I need to purchase this ticket?**
- **Will I be able to reuse the ticket if I cancel?**
- **What is the fee for making changes to my ticket?**
- **Do you offer discounts to frequent fliers? Students? Corporations?**

- May I use frequent-flier miles for upgrades?
- Is this the only airline that provides service to my destination?
- Will I have ample time (at least one hour) to make my connection?
- What are the luggage or security restrictions?
- Can I reserve the flight now and confirm later?
- Can you make my seat assignment now?

GETTING YOUR TICKET

When you make your reservation, request a seat assignment (although, depending on the airline's policy, you may need to do this instead at the gate before you board the plane). Many business travelers prefer an aisle seat toward the front of the aircraft so they can get off the plane right away and head straight to their meeting. If you'll be working during the flight, ask for a bulkhead or emergency-exit-row seat, since these usually have more room for spreading out paperwork.

Booking your ticket online is often cheaper and faster than booking a ticket over the phone. Always compare the lowest Internet fare with the lowest fare quoted by a ticket agent. Getting an e-ticket (an electronic ticket sent via e-mail) saves you the shipping fee airlines usually charge for sending an old-fashioned paper ticket, and it enables you to check in faster at many airports by using an electronic check-in. When checking in with an e-ticket, bring your confirmation number and the credit card you used to book the ticket.

> **GETTING IN AND OUT for less**
>
> *Consider flying into a secondary instead of a primary airport (e.g., Oakland instead of San Francisco, Burbank instead of Los Angeles, or Newark instead of Kennedy). Secondary airports are often just as convenient to your destination and far less congested. In addition, flights into these airports sometimes come at a more competitive fare.*

booking your hotel

When selecting a hotel for business travel, look for comfort basics—quiet room, good room service, central location—and business services—Internet access, meeting facilities, business center. The following questions address the many issues you may need to consider when choosing a hotel.

* **Is the hotel close to both the airport and the location where you'll be conducting business?**
* **Does the hotel provide shuttle service to and from the airport?**
* **What kind of business services does the hotel have—Internet access, A/V equipment, private conference rooms, business center? Is there a charge for using these services?**
* **Is there a restaurant, lounge, or bar in the hotel appropriate for meetings?**
* **Does the hotel offer a corporate discount?**

- Does the hotel offer parking? What is the charge?
- Is there public transportation near the hotel?
- What is the daily room rate? Does the hotel offer special weekly or monthly rates?
- Does the hotel partner with any frequent-flier programs?
- What are the check-in and checkout times? Does the hotel offer express checkout?
- What are the room-service hours?
- Does the hotel have a well-equipped fitness center, sauna, or pool with extended hours?
- Does the hotel offer spa services, a beauty shop, or a gift shop?
- Is there an in-house concierge?
- Do the rooms have kitchenettes or coffee machines?

* Are the rooms equipped with voice mail, fax machines, Internet service, writing desks, VCRs, or DVD players?
* Do the rooms have a separate phone line for fax and Internet access?
* Can I request a quiet room?
* Can I request a room that gets a lot of daylight?
* Can I request a smoking or nonsmoking room?
* Can I request a room close to the fire exit?

YOUR NAME, PLEASE

Always ask for the name of the person who assists you with your reservation, and jot down the time and date of your conversation. You'll find this information helpful if any problems arise during your trip.

Once you've settled on a hotel, you can ask the facility to fax you a confirmation of your rate and any special requests you've made. If you are not booking through your company's travel agency, you will usually need to reserve your room with a credit card. (When you check in you'll also need to provide a credit card, although most business hotels won't actually charge the card until you check out.)

KNOW YOUR limit

Before you travel, make sure your credit card limit gives you the spending power you'll need to cover all of your expenses. If not, simply call your credit card company and ask them to increase your limit.

HOTEL MEETINGS

You can save time and money by holding meetings at your hotel. Not only will it be more convenient for you but you'll also save yourself the expense of taxicab fare. Also, coordinating meetings at your hotel can give you a "home base" advantage when conducting business. Before arranging a meeting at your hotel, familiarize yourself with the hotel restaurant, bar, and lounge. Know the menus, the prices, the quality of service, and the ambiance. If you're using a hotel conference room, ask if the hotel can help you coordinate everything from coffee and donuts for a morning meeting to cocktails and appetizers for a post-meeting powwow. If the hotel's catering is too pricey, call and ask the concierge if there is a less expensive off-site alternative that he or she could help you find and book.

ground transportation

The rules for ground transportation are as follows: Keep it simple; don't wait until you land to find out how you're going to get to your hotel; and always choose the least stressful option. You'll be fatigued from the journey, burdened with luggage, and potentially disoriented in a strange city. Taking a taxi is probably your best bet. If you prefer a bus or train, make sure you are very familiar with the public transportation system, and choose a hotel that sits on a main public transportation artery. Whatever you choose, remember that your goal is to focus on business rather than spending time trying to figure out how to get from place to place.

If you are in your element when navigating and driving in a new city, then by all means rent a car—just be sure to plan for parking and traffic. When booking a car, stick with your company's preferred rental company and join their frequent-user club. Here are a few questions to ask when reserving a car:

booking your trip

- What is the least expensive car available?
- Do you have a weekly rate?
- Do you offer corporate discounts?
- Is there a mileage charge? If so, what is it?
- How far is your rental office from the terminal?
- Can the car be left at the hotel? If so, what is the charge?
- Can it be dropped off in a different city? If so, what is the charge?
- What is your insurance fee?
- What features does the car have?
- What is the confirmation number?
- What is my confirmed rate?

maximizing perks

Traveling for business can sometimes allow you to accumulate frequent-user benefits that you can cash in for your personal use. Perks abound for the savvy frequent traveler, but you have to do some of the legwork yourself. This involves enrolling in clubs and award programs, finding good credit card deals, and always asking for what you want. Here are a few tips for maximizing perks.

SOME TIPS ON club membership

- ★ Keep track of your points! Don't rely on the club to always keep an accurate record.
- ★ Have other members of your family join and accumulate points.
- ★ When joining any club, check to see if affiliate companies match your firm's preferred hotel chain, airline, or car rental company.
- ★ Keep an eye on tie-ins with sister companies, such as hotels or car rental companies, which yield lucrative points when you book with both.

CLUB MEMBERSHIP

Membership definitely has its privileges. Being a member of a hotel's or car rental agency's frequent-user club will allow you to earn points or miles that you can then apply to future purchases, and it will also earn you special perks, such as expedited hotel check-in and rental-car upgrades. Whether you're taking the train, driving in a rental, or flying the friendly skies, if a frequent-user rewards program exists, join it. Affiliate programs and strategic partnerships can get you even more perks. Find out what restaurants, car rental companies, hotels, and retail stores your club has partnered with so you can maximize your points and benefit from their discounts. Check into clubs that allow you to use your miles with several airlines rather than just one. The frequent-flier program market is crowded and competitive. So don't be shy—join more than one club, and ask lots of questions.

CREDIT CARDS

If you will be paying for your own business travel expenses, get a credit card you plan to use specifically for business expenditures. Look for a credit card linked to a frequent-flier program, so that any purchases you make will earn you miles. Some credit cards operate on a point system. Points on a card can provide you with bonuses such as free upgrades, free nights at a hotel, or whatever promotional freebie is being offered at the time.

UPGRADES

Always ask if it's possible to receive an upgrade to a nicer car or a better class of travel. If you don't ask you won't receive! If you can't afford to pay for an upgrade, try using your frequent-flier miles or points. Ask how much it would cost to get you sufficient miles to upgrade. It may be worth it to spend an extra hundred bucks for a first-class seat so you'll get to your destination feeling rested and relaxed. And sometimes, if you're really lucky, a ticket agent will even upgrade you for free if the flight is nearly empty or just because he or she is feeling like doing someone a favor.

It's easy to plan a trip online. To simplify your booking, use an all-in-one travel service to quickly reserve flights, hotels, car rentals, or vacation packages.
The Top 5 Travel Sites are:
1. Expedia.com
2. Orbitz.com
3. Travelocity.com
4. Uniglobe.com
5. Int.net (Internet Travel Network)

When booking a trip online, always research several travel sites before you book anything. Don't forget to check the airlines' own Web sites regularly, sometimes there are hidden deals last minute. Always print out reservation confirmation pages and take them with you on the trip. Hard copies work wonders if you're being stonewalled at the rental car counter or hotel check-in desk. Don't book online with Web sites that don't give you one. Lastly, be sure to join a site's "Fare Watcher" service. This invaluable update alerts you when particular fares go up or down $25, or when it falls below a price point you had bid on.

INTERNET
tips

before you go

003

It's now just days before your departure. You've booked your flight and confirmed your hotel reservations. You understand the purpose of your trip and you've familiarized yourself with your destination. Now it's time to prepare your office, home, mind, and body for your trip. This chapter will offer advice and checklists to help you get organized and energized before you go.

preparing your office

There always seems to be so much to do at the office before a trip—letters that need to be written, proposals that need to be edited, telephone calls that need to be returned, and work-related materials that need to be packed. But you don't need to scramble like a lunatic the day before you go. Instead, several days before you're due to leave, make lists of things to do and to pack, and attend to each item, either by doing it yourself or delegating it to a coworker. Use the Preparing Your Office Checklist on pages 52–53 to help you accomplish all of your pretravel tasks.

ORGANIZING AND DELEGATING YOUR WORK

First, take some time to figure out what needs to be done both before you go and while you're away. Prioritize each task according to deadline or urgency. Once you've made a list of the things that will need to be done, separate them into a few categories by asking yourself the following questions:

✳ What items will need my personal attention before I leave?

These are the tasks that you and only you can do, such as recording a new outgoing message on your voice mail, downloading information from your computer, or signing checks. Creating a file folder

---

INTERNATIONAL TRAVEL AND cell phones

Many cell phone companies offer GSM phones that allow you to make and receive calls all over the world through a pre-paid SIM card. These phones can be used throughout the world and are a great accessory if your business takes you out of the country frequently. For details on GSM phone services, including roaming, visit the Web site of the phone company in question.

While GSM phones are certainly convenient, their fees can be costly. When you are traveling abroad, the best way to keep the phone costs down is to opt for a "pay as you talk" phone. Most cell phone companies abroad offer this service. When out of the country, you can purchase one of these phones and airtime credit at convenience shops, filling stations, and newsstands.

containing information and documents you'll need during your business trip, organizing your desk, and informing clients of your upcoming absence also fall into this category.

✱ What tasks can be done by my assistant or colleagues while I'm away?

Don't try to do *everything* yourself. Your assistant, your associates, and even your boss may be able to handle certain duties in your absence. Perhaps you can hand off that time-consuming project to an associate, or maybe your assistant can gather information you'll need for a report you'll be writing when you return.

✱ What tasks can I do while I'm away?

Responding to e-mail, jotting down ideas for a future client meeting, roughing out a draft of a memo or other document, and prioritizing your post-trip tasks are examples of things you can do while on the road. Traveling affords many opportunities for brainstorming and organizing your thoughts. While you're waiting to board your plane, flying to your destination, or riding in the taxi to your hotel, put that time to use and let your mind run free. You just might come up with a brilliant, innovative idea that'll wow your boss and earn you a promotion. At the very least, you'll be prepared to hit the ground running when you get back.

COMMUNICATING WITH COWORKERS

If your office associates will be handling work for you during your absence, make sure they know and understand what assignments you want them to carry out, and be clear about any deadlines they need to meet. Make detailed lists, including all necessary information, when handing a task over. Is there a high-maintenance client who'll need special atten-

> **get organized**
>
> *An efficient way to get organized is to make to-do lists. Set aside one notebook at your office and one at your home and jot down every pre-trip task or item that comes to mind. These handy lists will become essential aids, helping you remember everything from bringing the charger for your cellular phone to stocking up on your favorite moisturizer for that long plane ride. With each business trip you'll add a few more tasks or items to the lists until you've got a complete set of trip-preparation tasks. Consider entering these lists into your computer so that you can easily print them out before subsequent trips.*

tion while you're gone? Perhaps you can leave current project files or documents with a trusted coworker who can answer clients' questions on your behalf. Are your coworkers prepared to handle emergencies during your absence? Make sure you address these issues with the right people, just in case.

Keep your associates in the loop during your trip—schedule a daily check-in phone meeting or update them with daily reports via e-mail. And leave your itinerary and a cellular phone or pager number, both with an assistant or coworker and with your associates who will be taking on assignments, in the event that someone needs to reach you immediately.

A cluttered office or home is a nightmare to return to. Leave your office and home neat and in order, exactly the way you'll want to see it when you return.

tidy
38

PORTABLE office checklist

If you create a portable office kit ahead of time, packing your office materials becomes a piece of cake. Keep as many of the items listed here as possible in a small bag, so they'll be ready to go the next time you need to rush off on a business trip. All you'll need to do is collect the remaining items that pertain to that particular trip, and you'll be on your way. Just remember to restock your kit when you return.

If possible, pack your portable office kit in a bag that is small enough to fit in your carry-on case. Try to avoid bringing a separate carry-on bag for office-related items—remember that minimizing your luggage will help you maximize productivity.

Portable Office Checklist:
- ☐ Laptop computer
- ☐ Laptop cords and battery
- ☐ Cell phone
- ☐ Cell phone charger
- ☐ Calculator

- *Pens*
- *Notebooks*
- *Mini audio recorder and tapes*
- *Business cards*
- *Postage and office stationery*
- *File folders*
- *Blank overnight shipping slips*
- *Frequent-flier, car rental, and hotel membership cards*
- *Address book*
- *Handheld computer*
- *Calendar*
- *Agenda*
- *Project or client files*
- *Notes*
- *Itinerary*
- *Small bills and change for tips and phone calls*
- *Map and guidebook for your destination*

PACKING YOUR BRIEFCASE

Make a list of everything you'll need to bring from your office, including files, CD-ROMs, presentation boards, samples, and so on. Do you have a laptop or PDA? How about cellular phone attachments and charger? Do you have all the tools you'll need in order to make a smashing presentation—the right pens, clipboards, binder covers, and folders? Add them to the list. Consult the Portable Office Checklist on pages 48–49 to make sure you've got everything you need, and then pack all the items on the list in a bag or briefcase.

Next, make copies of every file, disc, chart, miscellaneous news clipping, or Pantone color card you need to bring along—and even those you think you might need. Make duplicates of critical files or documents you'll be bringing with you and leave them in an easily accessible location in your office, in the event that your luggage is lost or stolen. Organize these papers in your business-trip file or portfolio, and stow it in your briefcase before you leave. On the night before departure, triple check to make sure you have packed every last file, memo, and lucky pen on your list.

REVIEW YOUR GOALS FOR THE TRIP

Before you leave your office, ask yourself exactly what you aim to accomplish on this trip, both professionally and personally. Are your objectives and goals crystal clear? If not, review the answers to the questions you asked your supervisor or colleagues in chapter 1. Walk out of your office with a definite agenda. Tell yourself that you're going to get what you need and want from this trip.

preparing your office checklist

Customize this handy checklist and use it to prepare your office:

- [ ] *Meet with your supervisor (and possibly your assistant or colleagues) to review trip goals.*
- [ ] *Make lists of tasks to be done before you leave and while you're away.*
- [ ] *Prioritize items on lists.*
- [ ] *Delegate work to colleagues.*
- [ ] *Confirm all trip-related meetings.*
- [ ] *Inform clients of your trip and give them the name and contact information of a coworker who will be able to provide assistance in your absence.*
- [ ] *Sign any important documents*
- [ ] *Change outgoing voice mail message and activate automatic "out of office" e-mail feature.*
- [ ] *Leave colleague, assistant, or superior your contact information and itinerary.*
- [ ] *Make copies of documents you'll bring with you; leave one set visible on your desk or with an associate.*
- [ ] *Organize and pack files, documents, discs, and CD-ROMs.*
- [ ] *Transfer essential files to your laptop.*
- [ ] *Obtain and pack company credit card, emergency credit card, checks, petty cash envelopes, manila envelopes to hold receipts, and/or expense reimbursement forms.*

- ☐ Check credit card limits.
- ☐ If you're traveling to another country, exchange at least US$100 for the currency of your destination, have at least US$200 in travelers checks, and bring a currency converter.
- ☐ Pack essential office supplies, such as a lucky pen, a calculator, notepads, and business cards.
- ☐ Make and leave copies of your ID, passport, and credit cards.
- ☐ Clean off your desk.

What else do you need to do:

- ☐ _____
- ☐ _____
- ☐ _____
- ☐ _____
- ☐ _____
- ☐ _____
- ☐ _____

preparing your home

There's no place like home, especially when you're away from it. So that you can concentrate on accomplishing the goals of your trip instead of worrying about your cat while you're gone, make sure your house, pets, and plants are well cared for in your absence. In this section you'll find valuable tips to help you take care of all of those little domestic details before you leave.

ARRANGE FOR A HOUSE SITTER

If you'll be gone for more than a couple of days and you live alone, have someone you trust implicitly keep things under control at your home. If you don't have a housekeeper or other hired help, coax a friend or trusted neighbor to check on your home daily, bring in the mail, tend to your pets, and water your plants. You can bake cookies or bring back souvenirs (and offer to return the favor at a later date) in exchange for such help. If your trip will take you away for more than a few days, then consider hiring a house sitter. A starving student or a bored retiree may be an ideal candidate for this job. Below are some things you can do to make sure your sitter is thoroughly prepared to care for your home:

★ **Write down specific instructions regarding pet and plant care.**

★ **Let your sitter know when the trash and recycling need to be put out.**

★ **If you have a security system, make sure your house sitter knows the code and how to operate the system.**

★ **Leave some cash ($100 or so) and a signed blank check to cover any emergency your house sitter may be need to address. To prevent a bounced check, put a cap on the check amount, either by writing the limit on the check itself (simply write "not more than X dollars" on the amount line) or by telling the house sitter what the limit is.**

In addition, make two lists of information to give to your house sitter. One list should have the phone numbers of emergency contacts, including an office associate, relative, family friend, lawyer, doctor, veterinarian, landlord, handyman, bank, and security company. The other list should have account numbers of credit cards you plan to bring with you, along with the credit companies' emergency phone numbers, in the event that your credit cards are lost or stolen. (Canceling credit cards can be a nightmare if you don't have this information.) Copy these lists and keep them with you while you're on your trip. It's a good idea to carry them on your person, perhaps in a pocket—but not in your wallet.

HANDLING MAIL AND DELIVERIES while you're away

★ If you'll be gone for more than a week, you might want to have your house sitter open your bills as they arrive in the mail and pay any that are due before you return. Leave a few signed checks for the sitter to use for that purpose.

★ Suspend all deliveries, including newspapers and packages delivered by shipping companies such as UPS and Federal Express. Just call the newspaper circulation department or the delivery company's toll-free number and ask for deliveries to be held until you get back.

★ Consider stopping your U.S. mail delivery altogether if you're going to be away for several weeks or months; the U.S. Postal Service will hold your mail until you come to pick it up.

Customize this handy checklist and use it to prepare your home:

- ☐ *Confirm house sitter.*
- ☐ *Create lists of emergency contacts and credit card account numbers.*
- ☐ *Create lists of house-, plant-, and pet-care instructions.*
- ☐ *Leave emergency cash and/or check for house sitter.*
- ☐ *Leave one set of keys with the house sitter and another with a nearby neighbor or friend.*
- ☐ *Pay bills.*
- ☐ *Stop mail or arrange for someone to bring your mail from the mailbox into your home.*
- ☐ *Suspend newspaper delivery.*
- ☐ *Toss out or give away perishable foods from your refrigerator.*
- ☐ *Water plants and leave food and water for pets.*
- ☐ *Take out trash and recyclable items.*
- ☐ *Turn off gas and unplug small appliances.*
- ☐ *Turn on an indoor and outdoor light (or attach timers to automatically turn on and off lights or television), close blinds and curtains, lock windows and doors, and arm your security system (if any).*

What else do you need to do:

- ☐ _____
- ☐ _____

preparing your home checklist

preparing your mind and body

What could be more important than feeling and looking great? Your inner and outer wellness during a business trip are critical to your success. The tips listed here will help you put your best face forward, maximize your vitality, and minimize stress, anxiety, and related ailments, so that you can put all of your energy toward the business at hand.

A week or more before you go, make appointments for any needed grooming services. Organize your favorite beauty products and stock up if you're running low. Buy toiletries in travel-size packages or transfer items such as shampoo, conditioner, and lotion to small plastic containers.

You'll want to guard against jet lag. If you'll be traveling to a different time zone, start to prepare your body three days before you leave. Begin by drinking water—lots of it. Decaffeinate your system by limiting coffee, tea, and sodas. Avoid drugs, alcohol, and junk food. Moisturize your skin; recycled, stale airplane air dries out skin quickly. Exercise daily to strengthen your immune system and reduce stress. And, most important, get plenty of regular sleep.

To keep your body relaxed and healthy and your mind focused and calm before you leave, try writing in your journal, soaking in a hot tub or bath, listening to music, treating yourself to aromatherapy, or getting a massage. A little pampering can work wonders on your spirit. You'll embark on your trip feeling renewed and energized.

If you're feeling anxious, try meditating. Begin by relaxing your body and clearing your mind. Breathe deeply and naturally. When worries or extraneous thoughts come up, notice them but don't focus on them. Instead, focus on a mental picture or a mantra. The manner and setting in which you meditate are entirely up to you. A few minutes of quiet meditation each day can give you a fresh perspective and a clearer focus.

When you are preparing to go on a business trip, don't underestimate the value of double checking your to-do lists. You'll reassure yourself that you have taken care of every last detail, allowing you to proceed to your destination feeling relaxed and confident. Knowing you are completely prepared will free your mind so that you can focus on achieving the goals you've set for your trip.

FIGHT jet lag

Did you know that a little light can go a long way to avoid jet lag? Get a "body-clock calculator" at better travel stores or online at www.litebook.com. This handheld, pocket-sized device calculates how much light your body will need during a flight and then delivers the exact light doses at the right intervals. Also, limit the nasty effects of jet lag by sleeping 8 hours the night before you go, avoiding caffeine and sugar, and taking an over-the-counter jet-lag pill before you board.

preparing your mind and body checklist

Customize this handy checklist and use it to prepare yourself:

- ☐ Make beauty and grooming appointments.
- ☐ Refill prescriptions if necessary.
- ☐ Stock up on basic toiletries and cosmetics.
- ☐ Write down your doctor's telephone number and put it in your wallet.
- ☐ Make sure your health insurance card is in your wallet.
- ☐ Take the time to pamper yourself a little.

What else do you need to do:

- ☐ _____
- ☐ _____
- ☐ _____
- ☐ _____

004

packing like a pro

Effective business-trip packing involves careful planning and practice. Strategizing about exactly what items to bring and how to bring them will eliminate a mad dash to the airport with a poorly packed and overstuffed bag, or a frantic call back home begging your house sitter to overnight an important item you forgot. When you are on a business trip time is always of the essence; packing skillfully will help you utilize your time most efficiently by allowing you to stay organized and focused on the goals of your trip. This chapter will show you the best ways to select and pack all the personal and business items you'll need, in addition to some "just in case" items.

plan before you pack

As we suggested in chapter 1, before you start packing make sure that you understand every aspect of your destination, from the climate to the dress code of the office where you'll attend meetings. Will you attend any formal functions? What's the weather like? What is the style of the people you'll be meeting with—formal and conservative, or casual and hip? Ask coworkers if they can give you an inside take on the personalities and styles of the people you will be meeting.

Check the weather forecast a few days before you go. When visiting a larger city, find out the local dress conventions. For example, people on the East Coast tend to dress up more when going out to restaurants or bars than do their counterparts on the West Coast. If you will be meeting with foreigners, it is wise to familiarize yourself with their customs, including the attire they consider appropriate and professional.

Asking yourself the questions below will help you get a clear picture of the environment of your trip—is it icy or balmy, hip or conservative, recreational or business only?

- **Where am I going?**
- **With whom am I meeting?**
- **What is the weather like?**
- **What is the tone of the trip (e.g., fun or serious)?**
- **What is the dress style of the people I'll be meeting?**
- **How long will I be staying?**
- **What specific items will I need?**
- **What can I live without?**

Next, take a visual walk through your trip from beginning to end and imagine what you want to wear. Try to imagine every meeting and activity, luncheon and dinner, workout and free moment relaxing in your room. Visualizing exactly what are you wearing in each scenario will help you decide what you will need to pack. Now you should be ready to begin identifying the clothing, toiletries, and personal items you'll need to bring along.

> **CREATE A MASTER checklist.**
>
> *If you'll be traveling frequently for business, you'll find it useful to create a packing checklist and save it on your computer so that it can be reused for subsequent trips. Include the basics: shirts, pants, skirts, undergarments, hosiery, shoes, pajamas, cosmetics, and personal items. If you always pack the same trusty items, such as a favorite crisp white shirt, a blue blouse that goes with everything, or a navy blazer that gives you a polished look, add these staples to your list. Calculate how many formal and casual shirts, skirts, pants, and undergarments you usually need per day. Then, next time you're headed out of town, packing will be a no-brainer.*

what to pack

Here are the four golden rules of packing: First, bring a versatile business outfit, a casual ensemble, and something fun that you can wear out on the town. Second, pack items you can mix and match—stick to a simple color palette when choosing clothing, shoes, and accessories so that each item can be paired with everything else. Third, pack clothing that can go from day to evening and will work for more than one occasion. Fourth, make sure the shoes you bring are not only stylish but also comfortable—you'll be miserable if you have to trek all the way to the airport gate wearing shoes that hurt your feet.

Review the list on pages 68–69 and check off all of the clothing and personal effects you think you might need for the specific trip you are taking. Figure out how many of each item you might need for each day of your trip, multiply by the number of days, and write that number next to the name of the item. Lay out all of these items, and then start editing. Think simple: Instead of bringing two pairs of jeans bring one.

Remove that second pair of heels and opt for a pair that goes with all of the clothes you're packing. When you're selecting toiletries and personal items, consider that your hotel may provide some basic necessities, such as an alarm clock, hair dryer, shampoo, and cotton balls. Keep subtracting clothing and personal effects until you have pared your gear down to the very basics—which should be all you really need!

> *Here's a tip for truly frequent flyers: Even when you don't have a business trip coming up, keep a bag packed and ready to go. Include basic color-coordinated clothing pieces and accessories that are versatile enough to be worn for business and casual occasions. Buy and pack doubles of all your key toiletry and beauty products—including a toothbrush, toothpaste, cosmetics, hair products, razors, perfume, prescriptions, and so on. Then when you get that last-minute call to jet, all you have to do is grab your bag and go. When you return from each trip, note which items need replacing and restock them right away.*

BE READY to fly

packing checklist

Customize this handy checklist and use it when you pack:

WARDROBE:

- ☐ *Business suit*
- ☐ *Dressy jacket/blazer*
- ☐ *Trousers/skirts/shorts*
- ☐ *Button-down shirts*
- ☐ *Cardigans*
- ☐ *Heavy sweaters*
- ☐ *Socks and hosiery*
- ☐ *Undergarments*
- ☐ *T-shirts*
- ☐ *Pajamas and slippers*
- ☐ *Necktie/scarf/hair accessories/gloves*
- ☐ *Belts*
- ☐ *Business shoes*
- ☐ *Dressy shoes/dressy purse*
- ☐ *Walking/casual shoes*
- ☐ *Workout attire/bathing suit*
- ☐ *Coat*
- ☐ *Rain jacket and umbrella*

PERSONAL ITEMS:

- ☐ *Alarm clock*
- ☐ *Wristwatch*
- ☐ *Travel sewing kit*

packing checklist

- [ ] *Toothbrush/toothpaste/mouthwash/dental floss*
- [ ] *Razor and shaving cream*
- [ ] *Deodorant*
- [ ] *Shampoo and conditioner*
- [ ] *Hair dryer*
- [ ] *Brush/comb*
- [ ] *Hair grooming products*
- [ ] *Lotion/sunscreen*
- [ ] *Lip balm*
- [ ] *Cologne/perfume*
- [ ] *Skin care products*
- [ ] *Nail clippers and file*
- [ ] *Tweezers*
- [ ] *Cotton swabs/cotton balls*
- [ ] *Vitamins*
- [ ] *Prescriptions*
- [ ] *Cold/sinus medicine*
- [ ] *Earplugs*
- [ ] *Glasses/contact lenses and lens solution*

What else do you need:
- [ ] _____
- [ ] _____
- [ ] _____

BRING ALONG a little bit of home

Seasoned business travelers often like to include something to remind them of home when packing for a trip. If you will be away for a lengthy time, you may want to bring a few photos of family members or friends that you can tape to your hotel-room mirror, or a family video that you can pop in the VCR when you're feeling homesick. Some business travelers like to use their time away from family to nurture and reconnect with themselves. Consider packing some candles, a few meditation books, or a yoga mat—whatever small items you use at home to help you relax. For other things you can bring to make your hotel room a relaxing retreat, see the list below.

- ★ *Journal or diary*
- ★ *Business or popular magazines*
- ★ *Book related to work*
- ★ *Book to read for pleasure*
- ★ *Meditation candles*
- ★ *Aromatherapy products*
- ★ *Yoga mat or stretch bands*
- ★ *Family photos or keepsakes (not irreplaceable ones)*

how to pack like you mean business

Because security and luggage restrictions have become more strict at all airports, before you pack check with the airline to determine the specific requirements for luggage size and weight. Here are some space-saving tricks that will help you pack like a pro, regardless of the type of bag you're using.

ROLLER-BAG PACKING TRICKS

Pack in layers. For the first layer, lay long garments like dresses and pants on the bottom, letting the pants legs or hems of dresses hang over the sides, and lay belts along the sides of the bag. For the second layer, lay flat any items that you don't want to arrive wrinkled, such as button-down shirts, cotton or linen garments, and T-shirts. For the third layer, lay apparel such as jackets, sweaters, lightweight garments, and the outfit you plan to wear first. Fold the pants legs or dress hems over the top of the third layers. Finally, put shoes and other bulky items along the edges, filling in any gaps.

GARMENT-BAG PACKING TRICKS

When using a fold-over garment bag, roll up undergarments, socks, T-shirts, and other small clothing items and place them in the outside pockets of the bag. Put shoes and a small toiletry kit in the larger pockets. Hang suits, blouses, skirts, and dresses in the main compartment of the bag. Depending on the size of your garment bag, you may be permitted to carry it on board and hang it in a cabinet (check with the airline to determine size restrictions).

DUFFEL-BAG PACKING TRICKS

The best way to pack a duffel bag is to roll each item of clothing individually and place it in the bag. Put bulky items like shoes and makeup bags along the sides or at the ends of the compartments.

DON'T LEAVE ANYTHING behind

> Whenever you're leaving one place or arriving at another, run through a mental checklist to remind yourself exactly where your essential travel items are: tickets, identification card, passport, credit cards, itinerary, important phone numbers, keys, wallet, and so on. This way you won't leave anything behind!

MORE PACKING TRICKS

★ Place the heaviest items at the bottom of your bag and the things you'll need right away on top.

★ When you pack and repack, make a habit of placing the items in the bag in the same order, so you'll be able to get to what you need quickly.

★ Stuff socks into shoes and put each pair of shoes into a canvas shoe bag or plastic bag.

★ Roll up sweaters and undergarments and slip them into the corners of your bag or suitcase.

★ Fold pants, shirts, skirts, and dresses as little as possible. When you must fold, do so along the seams. Always button buttons and zip zippers.

★ To prevent spills during transit, put all liquids in screw-top plastic containers. Tape the tops of the bottles closed and place them in zip-lock bags or small plastic bags.

★ Save the plastic bags you get from the dry cleaners. When it's time to pack, hang any wrinkle-prone garments and cover them with the plastic bags. Then remove the hangers and lay the clothes, still in the bags, as flat as possible in your suitcase. Alternatively, put garbage or plastic bags at the bottom of the suitcase and between layers. This will prevent your clothes from wrinkling en route.

A WORD ABOUT Luggage

There are several types of luggage from which to choose, each of which comes with advantages and disadvantages. We recommend selecting a bag that is lightweight and versatile. But what's right for you really depends on your physical condition, your personal image, and how much you need to bring with you.

Duffel bags are often compact enough to count as a carry-on, but they can be heavy when fully packed—they've been known to cause shoulder pain.

Roller bags allow you to look professional and organized while saving your back. However, these bags are decidedly feminine in style, so they might not appeal to men who want to protect their tough-guy image. In addition, roller bags often have rigid sides and thus limit the amount you can pack in them.

Hanging garment bags offer lots of space for shoving in those last-minute items, and they also minimize wrinkles in garments. If you tend to worry that your favorite button-down shirt will arrive looking like it's been crumpled in a ball, or if you can't help packing what seems like your whole wardrobe, a garment bag is for you.

The best way to find a good piece of luggage is to do research. Look at the major luggage manufacturers' Web sites. Go to their retail stores and try out the pieces that appeal to you. While you're on your trip, look around and check out other travelers' bags. You might see one you like. If so, politely ask the person for the manufacturer's name and retailer.

005
getting there

Whether you travel to your business destination by train, plane, subway, or luxury car, you need to get there on time and utilize your time in transit efficiently. This chapter will help you arrange transportation to the airport or station, suggest ways to use your waiting time prior to boarding, and offer ideas for using your transit time to relax and rejuvenate.

transportation to the airport or train station

Your options for transport to the airport or train station are many. The method you choose will depend on the distance you need to travel, the traffic in your area, the availability of public transportation, and several other factors. Is long-term parking at your city's airport scarce? Does a commuter or subway train pull right up to the railroad station? Consider the logistics of getting to the airport or train station in your area as you read the information in this chapter. No matter which mode of transportation you choose, find out how long it will take you to get to the airport or station, call ahead to make sure your flight or train is on schedule, find out how early you need to arrive, and budget your time accordingly.

AIRPORT SHUTTLE

An airport shuttle will pick you up and get you to the airport on time. Airport shuttles are convenient, reliable, and generally cost-effective, with the price ranging from about $15 to $30 in most urban areas. If you choose to take a shuttle you won't have to worry about driving or parking. However, you won't ride alone; shuttle companies make money by transporting four or more passengers from one area at the same time. Additionally, the shuttle will probably pick you up several hours before your flight. This means you'll have to be ready to head to the airport much earlier than if you drove yourself or took a cab. Shuttle companies require advance reservations and generally accept credit cards and cash.

CAR SERVICE

When you use a car service, a hired chauffeur will pick you up at the time you request and take you where you need to go. Car services can be contracted on an ongoing basis or for one-time use. Some companies contract with car services to transport clients and high-level managers. Depending on the contract, you may be picked up in a town car or a limousine. By all means take advantage of the service if your company will pay for the cost of a hired car. If you'll need extra room to work, or if the ride to the airport or train station is more than an hour or two, opt for a limousine, if possible.

If you are responsible for the fee, consider splitting it with coworkers if you're traveling together. Sometimes a car service costs the same as a taxicab. Car services require advance reservations. Most accept credit cards and cash.

TAXICAB

Taxicabs are the most popular mode of airport and train station transport—a cab doesn't require advance scheduling and gets you there quick. In some busy urban areas you can even flag one down on the street. Most companies will accept credit cards and cash.

Remember, you'll need to record and itemize every single expense you make on this trip, from the latte you bring on board to your taxicab rides to and from the airport.

KEEP THOSE receipts.

PUBLIC TRANSPORTATION

Most cities have decent public transportation. However, considering the importance of getting to the airport or train station on time and the unpredictability of public transportation (even in an excellent transportation system), we suggest using this method of transportation only if the bus or subway will drop you right at the airport, if you are thoroughly familiar with the system, and if you are carrying only a lightweight bag or two. For example, in the Bay Area, BART is a great way to get from Oakland International Airport and San Francisco International Airport to San Francisco, but in the sprawling city of Los Angeles, where the dominant mode of transport is the automobile, public transportation may not be your best bet. Before taking public transport, call to find out the time of arrival at the airport and make sure your bus or subway line is running on time.

SELF-PARK

If you decide to drive your own car to the airport, you'll be able to choose between parking in the airport's long-term lot (often a shuttle ride away from the actual terminal) and using a "park and ride" service (which involves parking in a lot even farther away from the airport and riding in a van or bus to the terminal). Both options are convenient and allow you to be in control of your destiny when going to and returning from the airport. When your return flight lands you'll be able to drive directly back to your office or to a quick meeting. Do plan ahead and give yourself ample time to park and take the shuttle from the lot to the terminal. Most companies will reimburse employees for parking fees.

checking in for your flight

As soon as you arrive at the airport, you'll need to take care of three crucial details: checking your luggage, checking in, and requesting a seat assignment (if you did not do so when you purchased the ticket). To make the checking-in process go smoothly, keep your key travel papers in an easily accessible jacket pocket—you'll need your itinerary, ticket, picture ID, passport, and the credit card you used to purchase

GET A POCKET airport guide

If you travel a great deal and frequently find yourself in unfamiliar airports, consider purchasing a pocket airport guide. A good one will include diagrams of the layouts of the more than seventy major U.S. airports, showing ticket counter and gate locations, car rental offices, and baggage claim areas. Then, when you're flying to a new airport, you can refer to the airport guide; when you arrive you'll already know exactly where you need to go and how to get there.

your seat (if you're using an electronic ticket). Keep these items readily available at all times, especially when checking your luggage, going through the security checkpoint, and checking in at the gate.

If you have luggage to check and you are being taken to the airport by a shuttle, a taxicab, a hired car, or your best friend, you'll want to take advantage of the friendly skycap. Upon pulling up to the curb, unload your luggage and give it to the skycap, who will check your bags and send them into the terminal to be loaded onto your plane. For security reasons, the skycap will need to see your ticket and your picture ID. Note that a skycap cannot make seat assignments; if you do not already have a seat assignment, you'll need to do this at the gate or check-in counter. Don't forget to tip the skycap.

If you can't take advantage of the skycap's services, you'll need to stand in line in the terminal to check in your luggage. The agent at the counter will also make or confirm your seat assignment and give you a boarding pass. You may want to ask the agent some or all of the following questions:

- **Can I change seats at this time?**
- **Can I be assigned a bulkhead seat or an emergency-exit row?**
- **Is the flight on time?**
- **How crowded is the flight?**
- **Can I upgrade to business or first class?**
- **Is my connecting flight (if any) on schedule?**

Once you have checked your luggage, either with the skycap or the ticket agent, you'll need to proceed to the gate from which your flight will be departing. If you need to confirm the gate number for your flight, check the information screens, located in central places throughout the terminal, that display departing and arriving flight information. Look on the departing flights screen to find your flight and its corresponding gate number. Then follow the signs posted in the terminal and head for your gate. Try to get to the gate itself at least forty-five minutes before your flight is scheduled to leave, since some airlines begin the boarding process as much as thirty minutes before departure time.

At the gate, check in with the agents at the counter. The agents will assign you a seat and give you a boarding pass if you have not yet received one. Find out when they expect to begin boarding, so that you can know approximately how long you'll be waiting before you need to get on the plane.

to check or not to check baggage

Few things are more infuriating than arriving at your destination only to learn that your bags did not. And even when your luggage does arrive when you do, squeezing into a crowd of tired travelers to wait for your bags to appear on the baggage carousel can really slow you down. Because you need to travel fast and light, try to bring carry-on luggage whenever possible. Never check essential items; always carry important documents, business files, materials you'll need for meetings, and your laptop computer on the plane with you.

I've checked in . . . now what?

Now that you've checked in, you may have some time to relax and take a little breather. Airplane travel can quickly dehydrate you, so drink a lot of water prior to flying and during your flight. It's a good idea to carry a bottle of water with you. Decongestant medicine, moisturizer, lip balm, and earplugs are also useful items to have with you. You can pick up any of these items, in addition to magazines, books, and snacks, at the kiosk near your gate prior to boarding. Keep your boarding pass in a safe but accessible place and don't leave your belongings unattended.

USING YOUR PREBOARDING TIME EFFICIENTLY

If you are early, or if your flight is delayed, use the time to organize your thoughts and your plans—check voice mail, check in with the office, confirm meetings, confirm car rental and hotel reservations, go over your meeting agendas, and so on. If you have a laptop, write letters or memos, check e-mail, or pay bills.

Customize this handy checklist and use it before boarding the plane:

- ☐ *Buy water and other necessary items at kiosk.*
- ☐ *Check voice mail.*
- ☐ *Call the office.*
- ☐ *Confirm meetings.*
- ☐ *Confirm rental car and hotel reservations.*
- ☐ *Write memos, pay bills, or check e-mail on your laptop.*

What else do you need to do:

- ☐ _____
- ☐ _____
- ☐ _____
- ☐ _____
- ☐ _____

preboarding checklist

AIRLINE CLUBS

If you simply hate to wait at the gate, then hightail it over to the closest airline club. Ah, instant airport sanity! Airline clubs can provide relaxation and comfort to harried business travelers. These clubs, once men-only lounges where businessmen smoked and drank, are now considered by many to be the single best investment a frequent traveler can make. No longer smoky bars, airline clubs today are business facilities that offer travelers a much-needed refuge from loud flight announcements, greasy-smelling fast food, and chatter of other waiting passengers. Most clubs come complete with conference rooms, fax and copy machines, telephones, Internet access, overnight shipping drop-off boxes, and other business necessities. Some clubs even offer showers and gyms. Many clubs are staffed with attendants who will secure boarding passes and seat assignments, help make travel changes and confirmations, and assist with other business-travel needs.

Once upon a time business and first-class travelers could enjoy the use of airline clubs free of charge, but now most clubs are available only to those who pay an annual membership fee. Some airlines offer day rates, and most will allow travelers to put their frequent-flier mileage toward the annual fee. Some airlines permit passengers flying business or first class to international destinations to use the club for free when departing. Certain platinum credit cards will offer you a free airline club membership—check with your credit card company to see if it partners with a certain airline for this service.

Many clubs have reciprocal arrangements with one another. However, club privileges don't always transfer from one club to another. Call the airline you're flying with and find out ahead of time whether you will be able to use your club membership. Or consider enrolling in a network that offers multiple club membership. Day rates range from $30 to $100—well worth the expense if you find yourself with an eight-hour delay!

on board

Prior to settling in your seat, take out any items you may need in transit, so that you don't have to disturb your neighbors by getting things out of your bags in the overhead compartment during the flight. Medications, cosmetics, and other products you may need in flight should be kept in an easily accessible bag or pocket. Remember to keep your magazines, file folders, or laptop out, too. If you've brought only a small carry-on bag, tuck it under your seat instead of cramming it in the overhead bin.

It's no secret that planes are usually quite cramped and passengers are situated too close to each other for comfort. So when you're working during the flight, be aware of your neighbors. There is no guarantee that the guy next to you isn't reading everything on your laptop screen. Many corporations request that employees avoid using their company laptops in public areas, in order to protect privileged or valuable information. If the seat next to you is empty and you can turn your laptop so that no one can see it, then you may be able to work in privacy and avoid disturbing other passengers.

Time spent in transit may be best used doing nothing at all! Perhaps you will benefit from using this time to write in a journal, read a new book, or go over a meeting agenda in your mind. Or maybe what you really need is a restorative nap. Ask your flight attendant to bring you a blanket, snuggle up (with seat belt fastened), and drift off to sleep. When you arrive, you'll be rested and ready to begin the business of your trip.

006
you've arrived

Once your plane touches down, your highest priority is to get to your hotel so you can settle in and get down to business. With a little preparation and forethought you can make your trip from the airport go smoothly and set the tone for the entire trip. This chapter will discuss your transportation options to the hotel and explain how to get the most out of your hotel stay.

transportation to the hotel

If you haven't already arranged for transportation to your hotel, ask your flight attendants what mode of transportation they suggest for the particular city you are going to; being frequent travelers themselves, flight attendants may be able to give you great tips on getting around and other aspects of travel in cities they visit regularly.

Many major hotels offer their guests free shuttle service directly to and from the airport. Call ahead to see what the hotel's arrangements are, or ask for your hotel's shuttle pickup location at the information desk near the baggage claim area. Taxicabs are almost always readily available at any airport or train station. Be sure to ask for a receipt so you can be reimbursed for the fare—and don't forget to write the tip on the receipt! Public transportation is an economical option, but we recommend using it only if you have ample time, are familiar with the city you are visiting, know the public transportation routes and schedules, and are carrying minimal luggage.

If you've reserved a rental car, head directly to the rental desk. Many are located next to the baggage claim area. If you must take a shuttle to the rental car lot, utilize the time spent in the shuttle by calling to confirm your upcoming appointments, checking in with your office, or checking your voice mail. Once you pick up your car, you'll probably need to head directly to your hotel. See if you can park your rental car in the hotel garage; this option is much cheaper, more convenient, and usually faster than using the hotel valet.

A TIP FOR HASSLE-FREE car rental pickup

Once you land, use your cell phone to call the car rental company. Let them know that you have arrived and are en route to their desk; ask if they could please have your rental paperwork ready to go. If you are a frequent renter, consider joining the car rental company's frequent-user club for extra services such as faster check-in.

If you discover any problems with the car (e.g., the car is not clean or spacious enough, or it isn't the specific vehicle you booked), then don't hesitate to request a change. The car rental company should give you an upgrade or a discount as compensation for the inconvenience.

checking in at the hotel

When you arrive at the hotel, register at the front desk. If you are a member of the hotel's preferred-guest club, ask the clerk how many points you will earn during your stay and what perks your current total points will get you. Always ask for an upgrade upon arrival; if the hotel is not fully booked, front desk clerks will often upgrade regular customers or club members for no added charge. Even if you are not a club member, let the employees at the front desk know that you'll be conducting business during your stay and would appreciate their assistance toward this end. If your hotel has a business center, ask for a complete tour, so that you'll be familiar with its equipment and services should you need to use the facility during your trip.

Once you have received your room key, ask to speak with the manager. Introduce yourself and let him or her know that you (and possibly your colleagues) expect to be staying at the hotel regularly. Making this introduction may lead to your receiving special service or an upgrade in the future. Also, take a moment to introduce yourself to the concierge and let him or her know that you may need his or her services during

HOTEL tipping

Aside from the usual tipping suspects—cabbies and drivers and wait staff—hotel staff should also be tipped, especially if they accommodate special business requests. You may tip the hotel concierge $5 to $20 for helping to arrange a meeting or luncheon. You may tip the business center manager $5 a day if this person goes out of his or her way to assist you. While it is not customary to tip the hotel manager, you may write a thank-you note or send a bouquet of flowers once you return home if he or she makes your stay more pleasant. Tip the doorman and the bell staff $2 per bag or service performed. When tipping housekeeping staff, leave $2 to $3 cash on the desk or bedside table before you check out.

If handing over cash tips makes you feel uneasy, you may place the cash in a small envelope, write the intended recipient's name on the envelope, and leave it for that person with instructions at the front desk.

your stay. Giving a tip to the concierge at this time will encourage prompt service when you require his or her help later.

Make sure everything in your room is in working order. Are your lights, television, voice mail, fax, phones, and Internet connections functioning properly? If any equipment is damaged, ask for replacements. And if the room you are given is too noisy, too small, or in any way undesirable, don't be shy—ask for a different room immediately. You are there to conduct business, and a comfortable room will be essential to your ability to get business done.

GEARING UP

You're now settled in your room. Your next task is to gear up for the business of your trip. First, set up your work materials in one area of your room, either at the desk or table, near the phone and Internet connection. You'll want to arrange your work area so that you can easily find whatever files, papers, and other items you might need. Plug in your laptop and cell phone charger. Get out your pens, notepad, and other supplies. This will be your office for the next few days, so make it as easy to use as possible.

Next, check in with your office and home, and let your contacts know that you've arrived safely. Check your office, home, and cell phone voice mail and return urgent phone calls, provided it's not too early or too late. Check your e-mail. Jot down any ideas that may have come up while you were in transit. Start your expense log and organize your receipts.

Finally, confirm any upcoming meetings or review with the concierge the details of any off-site meetings you plan on hosting. If you will be hosting a meeting on site, speak with the sales office and confirm that all of the elements for the meeting are in order, including tables and chairs, presentation materials or samples, beverages, food, and decor.

checking-in checklist

Customize this handy checklist and use it when you check in at your hotel:

- ☐ *Register at the front desk; ask about points and perks you will receive during your stay.*
- ☐ *Introduce yourself to the manager and concierge.*
- ☐ *Ask to take a tour of the business center.*
- ☐ *Do a room check; make sure everything is in working order.*
- ☐ *Confirm upcoming meetings.*
- ☐ *Check in with your office and home.*
- ☐ *Check voice mail and e-mail.*
- ☐ *Confirm any meeting arrangements made with concierge or sales office.*
- ☐ *Organize receipts.*

What else do you need to do:

- ☐ _____
- ☐ _____
- ☐ _____
- ☐ _____
- ☐ _____

home away from home

After you've gotten your urgent business tasks out of the way, you'll want to make your room as comfortable as possible. A soothing, nurturing atmosphere is important because when you're feeling relaxed and calm, you're more likely to feel confident, think clearly, and make smart decisions, which are key factors in the success of your business trip. While your business hotel may provide temporary living quarters that are clean and serviceable, perhaps even luxurious, not all hotels pass the comfort test on every level. You can add what's missing by setting up your room to look, smell, and feel as calming to you as possible, so that you can start and end each day of your trip in an environment that relaxes and cheers you.

The comforts of home are portable. To add familiar touches to your room, bring your own alarm clock, aromatherapy candles, incense, or special pillow. Simple items such as a family photo, a soothing CD, or even your favorite snacks can make you feel at home in an unfamiliar place. Ask for extra towels or toiletries if you need them to help you feel more comfortable. At the end of a long day of meetings, pop in a CD from home, light a vanilla candle, or take a foamy bath. If you treat yourself well, eat healthful food, get enough sleep, and relax in your home away from home, you'll be at your most effective and ready to take on any challenge during your trip.

Before going to bed, take a look at the day ahead of you. Set your alarm clock, or schedule a wakeup call with the front desk. Leave yourself plenty of time to get ready in the morning, eat breakfast, and get to your appointment. Make sure your briefcase is packed with all of the things you will need. Be thorough, and take your time. You'll sleep better knowing you're prepared for next day's work.

CALL ON THE CONCIERGE
before your meeting

Consider speaking with the hotel concierge well before setting out for your appointment. He or she can help you by giving you driving directions to your meeting, recommending the best public transportation route, or calling you a cab. He or she can also give you estimated travel times.

out and about

007

Most of the preparation for your trip is done before leaving home. You've defined your goals, and asked colleagues about the company and the people with whom you're meeting. You've mapped your destination, meetings, and business lunches. The time has come to accomplish what you set out for. And, although you probably won't have a great deal of free time between meetings, it might be possible to squeeze in a little bit of fun. It's okay to combine work with a little play, as long as the play doesn't take you away from the business at hand. This chapter offers a few general pointers on conducting your business and some suggestions for having fun while you're at it.

going about your business

You've made it to your destination, now it's time to get down to business. There are as many types of meetings as there are people in the world. The nuances of the strategies you will employ in accomplishing your goals will depend largely on what those goals are and the personalities of those with whom you are meeting. Still, there are a few, cardinal rules of etiquette that are always good to bear in mind.

★ Be prepared

Make sure you bring along everything that you will need. This includes the name and contact information for the person with whom you're meeting, directions, pen and paper, your business cards, credit card, cell phone, laptop, and any documents you might need for your appointment. In addition, be mentally prepared. Review your agenda, your strategies, and your ultimate objectives.

★ Be on time

Give yourself plenty of time to get to your destination. Of course, everyone is late once in a while. When it happens to you, be sure to call in advance of your original meeting time to apologize and to alert the person with whom you are meeting to your late arrival.

★ Be courteous

Even if your meeting plans involve tough negotiations, being courteous is the first step toward a good business relationship. Treat your counterpart as you would like to be treated.

★ Be prepared to pay

This rule comes into play when your meeting involves a meal or drinks. In the strictest of terms, the person who does the inviting should do the paying, but there are numerous variations on this rule across all industries. It's simply best to have your credit card on hand at all times.

If you're on a fact-finding trip, you may be required to generate a report upon your return. In this case, your notes will be an indispensible resource. You may think that you'll remember everything, but in an unfamiliar environment with potentially new faces, it's amazing what can go in one ear and out the other. Write it down.

TAKE notes

taking time to play

If you have some downtime in the evening, take advantage of it! Try not to do any work and instead treat yourself to an enjoyable evening. If you're visiting a big, exciting city check the local paper for events and concerts. Choose something that is easy to find, affordable, and nearby. Ask the hotel concierge for a recommendation for a local spa or fabulous restaurant. Visit the city's art museum. Find a great sports bar where you can watch a game and chat with locals, or check out a movie. Find yourself in a stunning locale? Let nature inspire you: take an early morning walk, or rent a bike (or even a pair of roller blades) and go for an invigorating ride. If you prefer to stay in, rent a movie and order a sumptuous meal from room service.

The most successful business trips include a splash of fun. Even taking only thirty minutes a day to indulge yourself will make a difference in your serenity and self-confidence. The positive outlook that results will certainly will help you to accomplish more.

SHOPPING

If you have the time and energy and you enjoy shopping, check out local festivals, seasonal sales, and outlets if you come across them. Investigate a small town's local specialty shops or go to that huge shopping emporium you've always dreamed of visiting. If you're staying at a hotel adjacent to a shopping area with unusual boutiques and cute stores, consider purchasing a few early birthday or holiday gifts. If your business has taken you to the middle of nowhere, then consider yourself lucky—some of the best shopping can be done off the beaten track.

REST AND RELAXATION

Contrary to what you might think, rest, relaxation, and exercise can and should be a part of a well-planned business trip. Plan your sleep. Schedule workouts and meals. Drink plenty of water. Book a massage if you can afford it. If you put these basic needs on your schedule, you'll be more likely to take care of your body, which will in turn allow you to work with better efficiency.

Many hotels offer not only a full-service gym but also in-room yoga tapes or exercise machines. Some properties have an in-house spa or swimming pool. Those that don't may have an arrangement with a nearby gym, spa, or Pilates studio that allows guests to use the facilities free of charge or for a discounted fee. Ask the front desk clerk whether the hotel offers any special spa or exercise accommodations.

Here are some activities you might consider when you want to put a little fun and relaxation into your trip.

- ★ **Check out local festivals, concerts, or art shows.**
- ★ **See a movie.**
- ★ **Watch a game at a sports bar.**
- ★ **Take yourself out for a nice dinner.**
- ★ **Stay in, order room service, and rent a movie.**
- ★ **Take a long walk.**
- ★ **Rent a bike or roller blades.**
- ★ **Go on a hike and explore your surroundings.**

- ★ Do some early holiday and birthday gift shopping.
- ★ Explore small specialty shops.
- ★ Go to a big mall or outlet.
- ★ Book a massage.
- ★ Exercise.
- ★ Eat well.
- ★ Drink plenty of water.

008
coming home

Now that your business is done, you can head home. You are probably exhausted by now, so it is especially critical for you to stay organized and avoid getting overwhelmed. This chapter will offer tips for checking out of the hotel, getting home, evaluating the success of your trip, and slipping back into your regular routine.

before you check out

There are several things you can do to make the trip home as smooth and stress free as possible. If you'll be catching an early morning flight, you'll want to take care of these details the afternoon or evening before you leave. Read on for a complete discussion of these tasks.

CONFIRM TRANSPORTATION ARRANGEMENTS

Before checking out of your room, call your airline and confirm your flight departure time and seat assignment, if any. Will you need to allow time to return a rental car? If your flight is delayed, be sure to let the car rental company know that you will be arriving late, so you are not charged a late fee. Confirm your transportation to the airport, as well as your transportation home or to your next destination. Will a friend pick you up when you land, or will you take a taxi home?

LAST-MINUTE BUSINESS

While you still have access to the hotel business center or your in-room Internet connection, return any calls or e-mails that need prompt attention. Confirm any meetings scheduled for later in the day. And, while your experiences of the past few days are fresh in your mind, make a list of things to be done upon your return (if you haven't already done so), and organize any pertinent information gathered during your trip. For example, did a fellow businessperson give you a valuable tip? Write it down and make a note to send that person a thank-you letter or gift. Did you promise to follow up with an important contact upon returning to your office? Did you tell a colleague you would forward some information to him or her? Add these tasks to your to-do list. Making a commitment and following through demonstrates integrity, which can only enhance your reputation.

Seek out the hotel manager, concierge, front desk clerk, and anyone else who went out of his or her way to help you accomplish your goals. Offer these people your sincere thanks and a tip, if appropriate.

CALL YOUR OFFICE AND HOME

Check in with your office and retrieve any new telephone messages. Speak with your assistant or boss about any urgent matters that require your attention before you board the plane. Call your house sitter, a family member, or a friend and let that person know you're coming home. Give your sitter some time to clean up and make sure that your home is in order for your arrival.

before you check out checklist

Customize this handy checklist and use it before you check out of your hotel:

- ☐ *Confirm your flight and seat assignment.*
- ☐ *Confirm any meetings scheduled to take place after you land.*
- ☐ *Confirm your transportation to and from the airport.*
- ☐ *Complete any unfinished business.*
- ☐ *Write down information gathered during the trip; create to-do list.*
- ☐ *Check in with your office.*
- ☐ *Check voice messages; return any calls that require immediate attention*
- ☐ *Call your house sitter, a family member, or a friend to say that you're coming home.*

What else do you need to do:

- ☐ _____
- ☐ _____
- ☐ _____
- ☐ _____
- ☐ _____

checking out of the hotel

Express checkout is often made available to preferred-guest club members. Many hotels offer an easy checkout option via the television in your room. Familiarize yourself with this system, since it can save a lot of time and hassle when you're in a time crunch. If you use this checkout system the night before you depart, many hotels will send a receipt to your room first thing next morning. To save even more time, ask for a preliminary receipt to be delivered to your room the evening before you leave, so you can review and verify the charges and make corrections if necessary without risking missing your plane. In the morning, if you've used the express checkout system, you can probably

> *Will you be heading to the airport early in the morning? Pack your bag and briefcase the night before, leaving out only the clothes you'll wear and the toiletries you'll need in order to get yourself ready. After you're dressed and coiffed, you'll simply need to tuck your toiletry bag and pajamas into your suitcase and head out the door.*

PACK 'N' go

leave your key in the room. If not, plan to stop by the front desk on your way out to drop off your key.

Before you leave your room, double-check to make sure you haven't left anything behind—a hair dryer in the bathroom, shampoo in the shower, or a pair of shoes under the bed, perhaps. Be especially careful to check for any work-related materials you might have left. Don't forget to leave a tip for housekeeping. If the bellman helps you with your luggage, tip him as well.

A SECURE checkout

One way to simplify your review of your final hotel bill is to use a special code number when charging items to your room in situations where you can give a tip. This method allows you to verify many charges on your final bill because they will end in your special number. For example, choose the number 49. Whenever you charge anything to the room, such as a drink at the bar or lunch by the pool, calculate the tip amount that will make the total end in $.49, and add that tip to the charges. For example, if your room service bill is $25.00, add a tip of $4.49, so that your total is $29.49. If your charges at the bar come to $16.50, add a tip of $2.99; your total will be $19.49. Then, when you review your hotel bill, you'll know that the discretionary charges ending in $.49 were made by you. Consider it your little personal security system!

checking out checklist

Customize this handy checklist and use it when you check out of your hotel:

- ☐ Pack suitcase and briefcase.
- ☐ Check out via express checkout or in-room TV system.
- ☐ Request preliminary bill to be sent to your room the evening before departure.
- ☐ Double-check to be sure you've left nothing behind.
- ☐ Leave tip for housekeeping.
- ☐ Tip bellman.

What else do you need to do:

- ☐ _____
- ☐ _____
- ☐ _____
- ☐ _____
- ☐ _____

coming home

Home, sweet home. No matter how enjoyable or successful a trip has been, it's always a relief to return home. And if you planned well before you left, your home and office should be tidy and in perfect order when you arrive, making your return to familiar surroundings even sweeter.

UNPACKING

Despite how much you want to ignore your packed bag sitting on the floor, don't! Unpack as soon as possible. Don't wait until tomorrow, when so many other things will be demanding your attention, such as the tasks on your post-trip to-do list. Use your time now, however limited it may seem, to get organized and prepare to go back to work.

As you unpack, separate your clothes into a laundry pile and dry cleaning pile, and put these piles in plastic bags. When you head out to the office the next morning, you can drop them off at the cleaners. Put your toiletries back where they belong, and put your suitcase away.

Check your pantry and refrigerator and make a grocery list so you can stock up on all the items you tossed out before your trip. If any grocery stores in your town offer a delivery service, you may want to use it to buy some basics the night you return, so you'll have milk for your coffee or fresh fruit for breakfast the next morning.

ORGANIZING PAPERWORK AND RECEIPTS

Now is an ideal time to review the notes from your trip. Download or print all materials you'll need to bring to the office tomorrow. Add to your to-do list any follow-up calls and correspondence you'll need to address the next day. Review the business cards you collected and add to your address book the contact information for any business associates you met. Make a note of any extraordinary service you received at your hotel or perhaps at a restaurant where you held a meeting, and jot down a reminder to send a thank-you note.

Separate your receipts into three categories: expenses your company will reimburse you for, expenses they may or may not reimburse you for, and personal expenses you are responsible for but that may be tax deductible. Fill out your company's expense reimbursement form, if any, so you can turn in the form and your reimbursable receipts when you get to your office the next morning. Put receipts for your personal expenses in a file or manila envelope so that they're all in one place when it comes time to prepare your tax returns.

REVIEW YOUR TRIP AND REST

Now, before you get swept up in the flurry of work at your office, take an inventory of your business trip. Review every introduction, meeting, presentation, and travel arrangement. Make notes about what went well and what did not. Ask yourself whether you accomplished exactly what you set out to do. If you experienced setbacks or obstacles, list each of them and why you think they occurred. Think about how you managed an unexpected turn of events—could you have responded more effectively? Plan how you will report the results of your trip to your coworkers or supervisors. Reviewing the events of your trip will boost your confidence and prepare you to return to work the next day.

coming home checklist

Customize this handy checklist and use it when you return home from your trip:

- ☐ *Unpack.*
- ☐ *Separate garments that need to be laundered and dry cleaned.*
- ☐ *Make grocery list; order groceries if needed.*
- ☐ *Download or print any information off laptop to bring to office.*
- ☐ *Organize receipts and paperwork.*
- ☐ *Make notes about new contacts you made.*
- ☐ *Remind yourself to send thank-you notes if applicable.*
- ☐ *Make notes about your trip and rate your performance.*

What else do you need to do:

- ☐ _____
- ☐ _____
- ☐ _____
- ☐ _____
- ☐ _____

We hope that your business trip yielded all the results you and your company wanted. Perhaps you even exceeded the company's expectations, brainstormed ingenious ideas, or secured a new client! If you planned well, stayed organized, and took care of yourself along the way, then you undoubtedly had the most successful business trip possible.

Now that you're home, you deserve a rest. Let your business trip really be over. Congratulate yourself on a job well done, and allow yourself to unwind. Let your mind relax and release all thoughts of work. You can revisit them in the morning. It's time now to make yourself a cup of tea, watch some bad television, and get some much-needed rest.

Airports
  choosing, 30
  navigation through, 82, 84–85
  transportation to, 77–81, 93, 113
BART (Bay Area Rapid Transit), 80
Boarding, 90–91
  pre-, 86–87
Body preparation. See Mind and body preparation
Buses, 80
Car
  rentals, 36–37, 94, 95, 113
  services, 78–79, 93, 94
Carry-on bags, 85, 90
Check-in
  car rental, 95
  flight, 30, 82–85
  hotel, 96–100
Checklists
  home, 57, 124
  hotel, 100, 116, 120
  mind and body, 61
  office, 48–49, 52–53
  packing, 65, 68–69
  preboarding, 87
Check-out, hotel, 113–20
Clubs, membership, 38–39, 88–89
Communication, 44, 46, 114, 115. See also Checklists
Contacts, 33, 55–56, 105, 122
Credit cards, 18, 56
  carrying, 30, 34, 82, 106
  frequent-flier, 40, 88–89
Dehydration, 86
Departure gates and times, 84–85, 113
Discounts
  car rental, 95
  flight, 30, 38–41
  hotel, 31, 110
Duffel bags, 72, 74

Entertainment, 108–11
Exercise, 59, 110
Expenses
  airport shuttle, 77–78
  credit card, 18
  hotel, 97, 118, 119
  house sitting, 55, 56
  meeting, 106
  reimbursement, 16, 81, 93, 122–23
Flight(s)
  business class, 15
  check-in, 30, 82–85
  discounts, 30, 38–41
  on board, 90–91
  preboarding, 86–87
  preferences, 28–29
  reservations, 25–27, 28–30, 41
  seat assignment on, 15, 29, 84
Frequent-user programs, 38–40, 88–89, 95
Garment bags, 72, 74–75
Gates, departure, 84–85, 113
Gifts, thank-you, 97, 114, 122
Ground transportation, 36, 77–78, 80, 93. See also Maps
Home preparation
  for leaving, 54–57
  for returning, 115, 121–25
Hotel(s)
  check-in, 96–100
  check-out, 113–20
  concierges, 97–98, 103, 108
  discounts, 31, 110
  expenses, 97, 118, 119
  home comforts in, 101–2
  meetings, 35
  office setup in, 98–99
  preferences, 31–33
  reservations, 31–35
  transportation to, 93–95
International travel, 22–23, 44
Internet research
  on flights, 25–27, 30, 41